cultivating
CALM

cultivating CALM

AN ANXIETY JOURNAL

BRANDI MATZ, MSW, LCSW

ILLUSTRATION BY VERONICA COLLIGNON

ROCKRIDGE
PRESS

For general information on our other products and services or to obtain technical support, please contact our Customer Care Department within the United States at (866) 744-2665, or outside the United States at (510) 253-0500.

Rockridge Press publishes its books in a variety of electronic and print formats. Some content that appears in print may not be available in electronic books, and vice versa.

TRADEMARKS: Rockridge Press and the Rockridge Press logo are trademarks or registered trademarks of Callisto Media Inc. and/or its affiliates, in the United States and other countries, and may not be used without written permission. All other trademarks are the property of their respective owners. Rockridge Press is not associated with any product or vendor mentioned in this book.

Art Director: Jennifer Hsu
Art Producer: Megan Baggott
Editor: Marisa A. Hines
Associate Editor: Samantha Holland
Production Editor: Jenna Dutton

Illustration © 2020 Veronica Collignon

ISBN: Print 978-1-64611-779-6

R0

■ *contents*

■ *introduction*

Congratulations! You are one step closer to gaining clarity and control over your anxiety.

Everyone has a level of anxiety. It's a normal human emotion that we all share. Indeed, anxiety is actually what keeps us alive—its purpose is to alert us to danger. When we are standing at a crosswalk, for example, anxiety is what keeps us from walking in front of an oncoming bus. It's also what makes us pull our hand away from a flame. Anxiety is pretty important to have. However, when we have too much anxiety, or if it's irrational, it can interfere with our happiness.

Anxiety disorders are the most common mental health issue in the United States. Fortunately, anxiety issues also happen to be the most treatable. Over the last 20 years, I have been able to teach people effective strategies and ways to take control over their anxiety instead of it having control over them. I have seen how it can affect their daily tasks, their happiness, and even the people around them. I am grateful to have known so many people willing to share their experiences with me, and working together, we have improved all of our lives.

As an anxiety specialist, I often advise people to use journaling as a therapeutic tool to help them become more aware of and prioritize their emotions. Journaling can be a very effective way to process our feelings, clarify what it is that is causing our anxiety, and even identify where our fears are coming from. *Cultivating Calm* will present you with ways to focus on your emotions and connect them to your current feelings, thereby gaining a better understanding of yourself and your behaviors. Furthermore, by combining the journaling exercises with meditation, you will have the tools to reach your emotional goals and live the life you deserve to live. You will be able to take control of your anxiety and prioritize your emotions. You only get one life, so make it the best life. Enjoy your journey working through this book. You are worth it.

This book is designed for individual use as well as use in conjunction with therapy. It is by no means meant to replace professional help, however. If you are experiencing anxiety that impacts your daily life and/or ever have suicidal thoughts, it's important that you contact a therapist or psychiatrist.

HOW TO USE THE JOURNAL PROMPTS

There is no right or wrong way to journal, and there is no order that you need to follow. If you feel like one prompt isn't speaking to you in a particular moment, skip it and come back when you're ready. In each exercise, you will be asked to imagine yourself in a scenario and then to answer questions related to this scenario. If the situation doesn't speak exactly to your fears, then feel free to change it. There are no rules. The important thing is to just write about how you feel. Don't worry about spelling, language, punctuation, etc.—just write your feelings. If you need more room than provided, continue on a piece of paper. When you're done, go back and read what you've written. You may be surprised. The point of journaling is to become aware of your feelings and make connections between your emotions and behaviors.

With this knowledge you can begin to change what you are not happy with and set goals with a clear mind.

HOW TO USE THE MEDITATIONS

Meditation has been shown to reduce stress, lower anxiety, improve sleep, and increase overall health. There are several types of meditation, but for the purpose of this book, meditation will be used primarily to help you become more mindful and achieve a lower level of anxiety. Being mindful simply means to be present in the moment. Many people struggling with anxiety are focused on the future and "what if" thinking. We want to change that to "what is" thinking. Ideally, you will meditate daily. But do not put pressure on yourself. The important thing is that you are trying. Meditation is a practice, and it gets easier the more you do it. Just pick one meditation a day and set aside time in your schedule where you can be alone, even for just a few minutes. Find a comfortable, quiet space where you won't be interrupted. Turn off all devices and the television and pick a meditation that you would like to work on. Soon your sleep will be more restful and restorative, and your mood and anxiety will improve.

Warm wishes to you in your personal journey of self-improvement.

journal

PROMPTS

FEELING COMFORTABLE IN CROWDED SPACES

—

You gain strength, courage, and confidence by every experience in which you really stop to look fear in the face . . . You must do the thing you think you cannot do.

—Eleanor Roosevelt

PROMPT: Your friend has invited you to a concert. It is a large venue that will be crowded and loud, and you are unsure where your seats are or how close to the exit you will be. How does this invitation make you feel? Write about your fears and thoughts related to this type of situation. What physical changes do you notice? Is there a time when you have felt this way before?

_____

_____

_____

_____

_____

_____

_____

_____

_____

_____

_____

_____

_____

_____

_____

_____

_____

_____

_____

TIP: Being in a large crowd often presents an uncomfortable situation. However, the fear of the crowd or the unknowns does not need to prevent you from participating in such events. Ask yourself if you are afraid of the "what if" scenarios. Are you anticipating the worst-case scenario? Try to shift your thoughts to the "what IS." Focus on the facts and reality.

FLYING WITH EASE

—

Only when we are no longer afraid do we begin to live.

—Dorothy Thompson

PROMPT: Your in-laws are taking the entire family on a trip to celebrate their wedding anniversary. Attending is very important to your spouse or partner, but the destination requires a plane flight, and flying makes you uncomfortable. How will you respond? Write about your fears of flying. How does this fear affect those around you? What positives would come from your attendance?

_____

_____

_____

_____

_____

_____

_____

_____

_____

_____

_____

_____

_____

_____

_____

_____

_____

TIP: You are not alone in your fear of flying. It is common and real. Identify what it is that you are specifically afraid of. Educate yourself about what is normal when flying—busy airports, crowded airplanes, flight turbulence, etc. Will you allow your fear to keep you from time with your family, or will you face the fear and be stronger for it? Being educated about what to expect should help you identify which fears are irrational and reduce your stress.

STOPPING REPETITIVE, INTRUSIVE THOUGHTS

—

Happiness is not by chance, but by choice.

—*Jim Rohn*

PROMPT: You are lying in bed, trying to fall asleep, and images of your children getting hurt keep popping into your head. Identify what is in your control and what isn't. Write about how these fears have power over you. How much of these thoughts are your fears, and how much are they based in fact?

_____

_____

_____

_____

_____

_____

_____

_____

_____

_____

_____

_____

_____

_____

_____

_____

_____

_____

TIP: Everyone has intrusive thoughts. They are normal. These thoughts attack what is most important to you. What makes intrusive thoughts uncomfortable is how much attention you give them. Are you in control of your thoughts or are you allowing them to control you? You have the power to stop these thoughts.

KNOWING THAT MINOR SYMPTOMS ARE NOT A SERIOUS ILLNESS

—

Health is the greatest gift, contentment the greatest
wealth, faithfulness the best relationship.

—*the Buddha*

PROMPT: You watched a TV show that told the story of a girl who had to have emergency surgery due to a ruptured appendix. Later that night, you begin to feel a slight pain in your side. Although you attempt to ignore it, you think it may be getting worse. You are convinced you have appendicitis. Write down all the fears that you are experiencing. Then, pretend you are a caring friend. As that friend, what advice would you give yourself?

_____

_____

_____

_____

_____

_____

_____

_____

_____

_____

_____

_____

_____

_____

_____

_____

TIP: The body is complicated. It has many functions, and very often you feel its inner workings. Are you a relatively healthy person? Is there another reason that you could be having a pain? (A common mistake that people make is using the Internet to research their symptoms. This may only perpetuate your fears.) It's okay to pay attention to what your body is telling you as long as you can remain logical.

ACCEPTING THAT CONFLICT IS OKAY

—

In the middle of difficulty lies opportunity.

—*Albert Einstein*

PROMPT: Imagine you have dinner plans with a friend for Friday evening, that were made a few weeks ago. However, today a different friend invites you to a party that same Friday, and you accept the invitation because you are afraid to say no. Write about a time when you got yourself into a bind because you were afraid of the conflict of saying no. What happened? How did you feel afterward?

_____

_____

_____

_____

_____

_____

_____

_____

_____

_____

_____

_____

_____

_____

_____

_____

_____

_____

TIP: Conflict isn't comfortable for most people. However, it is a normal and expected part of every relationship. Most people who fear conflict use avoidance, but this does not make dealing with conflict any easier the next time it arises. The best way to face conflict is to slowly expose yourself to it. Try to have a difficult conversation with a safe person, or say no when your tendency is to please. Conflict doesn't always have to be messy, and it will get easier the more you deal with it.

CLEARING THE
CLUTTER ANXIETY

—

Get rid of clutter, and you may just find it was
blocking the door you've been looking for.

—Katrina Mayer

PROMPT: You walk into your house and see stacks of paper on every surface, shoes scattered on the floor, overflowing drawers, and heaps of unfolded laundry. What feelings does this elicit? How does having a cluttered home make you feel about yourself and your self-esteem?

_____
_____
_____
_____
_____
_____
_____
_____
_____
_____
_____
_____
_____
_____
_____
_____
_____
_____
_____
_____
_____

TIP: Clutter causes people to feel anxious, overwhelmed, and depressed. Your body responds to the environment that it is in. In order to get organized, it's important to not look at the entire project. Instead, break it into small tasks. For example, if you are donating old clothing, try filling one box and then just go through that box. Shift your mind-set from _what you are losing_ to _what items make you happy and reflect who you are._ Just take it one box at a time.

STOPPING THE OBSESSION WITH FINANCES

—

Don't let making a living prevent you from making a life.

—*John Wooden*

PROMPT: You think about money all the time. How much you have, how much you need, how you will retire. You find yourself checking your bank account balance several times a day. Think about what triggers you to worry about money, then make a list of those triggers. Identify what your ideal financial situation looks like. Where do your values about money come from?

TIP: Money is often associated with success and happiness. Nevertheless, people can have irrational ideas and fears about money. Being obsessed with the number in your bank account can be very distracting. It may be helpful to get a financial strategy from a professional who can provide a detailed plan for your financial goals and take the pressure off you, so that you can focus on living the life you are working so hard for.

BEING SOCIAL

—

We acquire the strength we have overcome.

—*Ralph Waldo Emerson*

PROMPT: You are watching your son's soccer game and are surrounded by the parents of your son's friends. They are all sitting together, talking and laughing. Write about what you are afraid of. Then list five compliments you have been given by others. How does being in this type of environment make you feel?

_____

_____

_____

_____

_____

_____

_____

_____

_____

_____

_____

_____

_____

_____

_____

_____

TIP: Being social should be something to look forward to, but for many, social occasions become dreaded events. It's important to have a plan in place before you go, in order to ease some of the anxiety. For example, plan on driving yourself instead of carpooling. This way you will always be in control of when you leave, eliminating the feeling of being trapped.

Furthermore, if you worry about what to talk about, remember that people are most comfortable talking about themselves. Ask people open-ended questions, such as "How was your day?" This will take the pressure off you to come up with something interesting to say.

BEING ALONE CAN
BE A GIFT

—

*I love to be alone. I never found the companion
that was so companionable as solitude.*

—Henry David Thoreau

PROMPT: You and your significant other have broken up. You are
single and living alone. Write about what being alone means to you and
why you feel this way. What fears or feelings does it bring up?

_____

_____

_____

_____

_____

_____

_____

_____

_____

_____

_____

_____

_____

_____

_____

TIP: Being alone does not mean that there is anything wrong with you. Use being single as an opportunity to develop a better understanding of yourself, without relying on someone else to make you feel happy. Take the time to observe others—the way they act, the way they treat others, and how they live their lives. Figure out what you can learn from what you see, then think about how you can make the things you admire in people part of your life. Being alone can be a gift if you allow it to be.

ENJOYING TIME
WITH YOUR
EXTENDED FAMILY

—

Be yourself; everyone else is already taken.

—Oscar Wilde

PROMPT: Imagine that it is your sister's birthday, and your mom is having everyone over to celebrate. You walk in the door, and your mom immediately asks why you changed your hair. Meanwhile, your dad is yelling something from across the room, and your aunt is asking when you think you will get married. Write about the roles your family members have, including yourself, and why you think these roles exist. Do you allow others' actions to control your mood? How do family gatherings affect you?

TIP: Spending time with family can be frustrating. But you can mentally prepare yourself for family visits by taking deep breaths and remembering that they are not in control of how you feel—you are. If you can change your mind-set, then time with your family may not be as anxiety-provoking.

You might try finding humor in the roles that people play. Think of it as a TV show you're watching. Or, if you feel as if you are getting frustrated or annoyed, quickly pretend you forgot something in your car, or you need your bag that you left in another room. Interrupt the conversation and politely excuse yourself. Then, take a few minutes to regroup. Hopefully, when you return, the conversation will have shifted to something else.

LEAVING THE HOUSE

—

We carry our homes within us, which enables us to fly.

—John Cage

PROMPT: You have promised yourself that you will leave the house today. You have a list of tasks that have piled up because of your avoidance. You plan to go to the dentist, pick up something at the post office, and go to the grocery store. Identify why leaving the house scares you so much. Are these fears based in reality?

_____

_____

_____

_____

_____

_____

_____

_____

_____

_____

_____

_____

_____

_____

_____

_____

_____

_____

TIP: People who fear having a panic attack in public often avoid leaving their homes to minimize this risk. However, avoiding the situation can make it worse. Try to make a realistic plan, and then take baby steps to achieve it. Each day, do one small thing that you are afraid of. When you are comfortable, try adding another. You can also learn relaxation breathing to help avoid panic attacks.

GETTING A HANDLE ON HOUSEWORK

—

Cleaning your house while your kids are still growing
is like shoveling the walk before it stops snowing.

—*Phyllis Diller*

PROMPT: You are trying to get ready to go out, and you can't find anything you are looking for. Your husband is in the shower and asks if he has any clean underwear. You can't tell which pile of laundry is clean and which is dirty. The sink is full of dishes and the bathroom's not clean. How do you feel when your house is messy? What prevents you from keeping it clean? How do you think your home affects your self-esteem?

_____

_____

_____

_____

_____

_____

_____

_____

_____

_____

_____

_____

_____

_____

_____

_____

_____

_____

_____

TIP: Feeling overwhelmed with keeping a house clean and organized is very common. It's difficult to get motivated when you are feeling overwhelmed. Nonetheless, you have to remember that your house did not get messy in one day, and it will not get clean in one day. Pick a small task each day and complete that. Don't let the idea of the entire project overwhelm you. Break it down into realistic, small tasks.

SPEAKING IN PUBLIC WITH CONFIDENCE

—

There are only two types of speakers in the
world. 1. The nervous and 2. Liars.

—*Mark Twain*

PROMPT: You have accepted the honor of giving a speech at your best friend's wedding. When you think about giving this speech, how do you feel? Are you excited or fearful? What are your fears? If you had no fear, how would you present this speech?

_____

_____

_____

_____

_____

_____

_____

_____

_____

_____

_____

_____

_____

_____

_____

TIP: Most people will be expected to speak in public at some point in their lives. If you have this fear, as most do, there are a few things you can do to help ease your anxiety and give a confident speech. Your audience is there because they want to hear what you have to say. Organize your speech and then practice a lot. Practice by recording yourself and by giving your speech to a friend. Leading up to the event, practice meditating as well as using common breathing techniques to slow your heart rate down. Drinking room-temperature water before your speech can help as well. If you speak from the heart, it will never be wrong.

LOWERING
DEBT ANXIETY

—

Getting knocked down in life is a given.
Getting up and moving forward is a choice.

—*Zig Ziglar*

PROMPT: Your credit card was declined at the store. At home, you find a pile of unpaid credit card bills that you've been pushing aside. Looking back, how did you get into this debt? Explore the timeline and list the emotional triggers that got you where you are now. Then, begin writing out a plan to stop overspending and pay off what you owe. In what ways do you avoid dealing with your finances?

_____

_____

_____

_____

_____

_____

_____

_____

_____

_____

_____

_____

_____

_____

_____

_____

TIP: Most Americans live with some sort of debt. Financial stress is a major contributor to depression and anxiety. Avoidance is the most common way that people deal with these stressors which, in turn, only perpetuates the problem. Get help if you are unable to get a plan in place. The first step is to stop avoiding the numbers and write them out. Figure out exactly how much you owe and begin to chip away at it. It will eventually get to zero if you stick with it. Be patient.

DRIVING
WITHOUT ANXIETY

—

Bravery is being the only one who knows you're afraid.

—*Franklin P. Jones*

PROMPT: You realize that it has been months since you have driven anywhere. Your fear of driving is affecting you socially and professionally. Make a list of what's holding you back from getting behind the wheel. Then make a list of all the positive things about driving—for example, *I am in control of when and where I go; I am alert and safe when driving.* What have you missed out on or what consequences have you experienced as a result of your fear?

_____

_____

_____

_____

_____

_____

_____

_____

_____

_____

_____

_____

_____

_____

_____

_____

_____

TIP: Some people are afraid that they will experience a panic attack while driving, and others are afraid of feeling trapped, or out of control. It's important to identify what your specific fear is and where it comes from. Slow exposure is the best way to deal with driving anxiety. Begin by driving in your driveway or in an empty parking lot. Once you are comfortable, go a little farther. You can drive anxiety-free—you just need to take small steps to get there.

BEING OKAY WITH BEING LATE

—

If you treat every situation as a life and death matter, you'll die a lot of times.

—Dean Smith

PROMPT: You have a meeting at 2:00 p.m. It's only 10:00 a.m., and you have checked the time and traffic 87 times. You keep thinking about what would happen if you were late. List all the things you are worried about and why being early is so important to you. Do you feel more in control when you think about the time? Is this rational?

_____

_____

_____

_____

_____

_____

_____

_____

_____

_____

_____

_____

_____

_____

_____

_____

_____

TIP: People have several reasons why they fear being late. Sometimes it is helpful to identify the worst-case scenario in order to put your fear into perspective and realize that the worst-possible scenario is really not that bad.

BEATING THE FEAR
OF DYING

—

People living deeply have no fear of death.

—*Anaïs Nin*

PROMPT: You have been daydreaming about death and dying. You begin to think about how you would die, what it would feel like, what your loved ones would experience, and about the existence of an afterlife. Write your own eulogy. What would you say about your life and how you lived it? What do you wish were different? How can you implement your insights into your current lifestyle to live your best life?

TIP: It is very normal to think about dying. Worrying about death isn't always a negative. It's what prompts your choices, like wearing a seat belt. If you are consumed with death, however, it can begin to interfere with your daily life. The exercise of writing your eulogy is to help you identify how you wish to live the rest of your life and to focus on the life you're living, not on your life ending.

CONQUERING WHITE-COAT SYNDROME

—

I am not afraid of tomorrow, for I have
seen yesterday and I love today.

—*William Allen White*

PROMPT: You have just received news that you landed the job you have been hoping for. The hiring manager tells you that all that is left for you to do is complete a physical. Write about your thoughts and feelings about going to the doctor. Then, write about the positive outcomes that could happen because of the doctor's visit. What is it that you are afraid of—a bad diagnosis, a procedure, the sterile room?

_____

_____

_____

_____

_____

_____

_____

_____

_____

_____

_____

_____

_____

_____

_____

_____

_____

TIP: People have differing reasons for being afraid of going to the doctor. It may help to bring a friend for support. You can call the doctor's office prior to your visit to ask what will be done at the appointment so you can be prepared if any tests or procedures will take place. Make sure you are comfortable with the doctor you are seeing and inform them ahead of time that you are experiencing anxiety related to the appointment.

DANCING AND LETTING GO

—

Of all the liars in the world, sometimes
the worst are our own fears.

—*Rudyard Kipling*

PROMPT: You are engaged to be married and your soon-to-be spouse is not only excited to have the first dance with you, but also to celebrate and dance together at the reception. Write about how you feel when you are dancing. What are some things you can do to feel more comfortable on the dance floor? How do you typically handle a social setting where you are expected to dance?

_____

_____

_____

_____

_____

_____

_____

_____

_____

_____

_____

_____

_____

_____

_____

_____

TIP: There is no right or wrong way to dance, yet a lot of people feel very uncomfortable and judged while on the dance floor. It can elicit feelings of insecurity and awkwardness. Just remember that people are probably more concerned with themselves than with you. Try to practice in front of a mirror or take a dance class. You can always watch videos of people dancing to get more comfortable with movements, but most of all, don't try too hard. Just move your body and let go of your fears.

TAKING A TEST WITH SUCCESS IN MIND

—

You don't have to control your thoughts. You just have to stop letting them control you.

—Dan Millman

PROMPT: You have an important test coming up, and you can feel your anxiety rising every time you think about it. Explore why you have test anxiety. What expectations do you have for yourself? Did you have a bad test experience? In what ways do you think you might contribute to the negative cycle? What do you tell yourself about test taking?

TIP: Many people perpetuate their test anxiety by repeatedly telling themselves that they will not do well. Try positive self-talk. Prepare for the test and make sure to meditate and do some deep breathing before your test to lessen your anxiety. There's no reason why you shouldn't do well. Believe in yourself.

EXERCISING WITHOUT JUDGMENT

—

You wouldn't worry so much about what others
think of you if you realized how seldom they do.

—Olin Miller

PROMPT: You have gained weight and know that you need to exercise. How does the thought of going to the gym make you feel? Write about fitness goals you have for yourself and how you can achieve them. What holds you back? Why did you stop exercising? Do you allow what others may be thinking prevent you from reaching your goals?

TIP: There are many anxieties related to fear of exercise. Some people fear that everyone will be judging them, and others are afraid that they don't know how to use the machines. You cannot allow fears to prevent you from caring for yourself. If you want to go to the gym, try starting out with a personal trainer who can show you how to use the equipment and give you a step-by-step plan, so you are not guessing. Focus on yourself and your goals.

NOT SWEATING IT

—

Rule number one is, don't sweat the small stuff.

Rule number two is, it's all small stuff.

—Robert Eliot

PROMPT: You are sitting in an important meeting, and you are scheduled to present next. You can feel the sweat start to bead on your face. You know that your shirt will start to show your perspiration soon. What is your first memory of nervous sweating? What do you think others think of you when they see that you're nervous? Is your nervous sweating related to your confidence level?

_____

_____

_____

_____

_____

_____

_____

_____

_____

_____

_____

_____

_____

_____

_____

_____

_____

TIP: Learning relaxation techniques such as meditation and deep breathing can help lower your heart rate, which in turn will help make you feel less nervous. Some practical things you can do are drink plenty of water, wear lightweight clothing with patterns or dark colors to hide your perspiration, and use a clinical-strength antiperspirant.

DETACHING FROM SOCIAL MEDIA STRESS

—

That fear of missing out on things makes
you miss out on everything.

—Etty Hillesum

PROMPT: You posted a picture on social media and have started getting likes and comments, then your phone dies. You don't have a charger and are now unable to check your status. How will you handle this? Do you allow social media to influence how you view yourself? How can you begin to detach your self-worth from social media?

_____

_____

_____

_____

_____

_____

_____

_____

_____

_____

_____

_____

_____

_____

_____

_____

TIP: Social media often breeds an environment of needing approval and can make many people feel as if they are missing out. One way to detach yourself from social media is to delete those apps. You may be less likely to check in if you have to log in every time. Or leave your phone in a different room or put it on airplane mode. Turning off notifications will also lessen the impulse to check in. Moreover, remember that people tend to post pictures that make them look good. Nobody has a perfect life; your self-worth is not related to how many likes you get.

MAKING THE CALL
THAT YOU FEAR

—

*To overcome a fear, here's all you have to do: realize
the fear is there and do the action you fear anyway.*

—Peter McWilliams

PROMPT: You have known for a few weeks that you are overdue for making a doctor's appointment or for phoning someone. All you have to do is pick up the phone and make the call. Instead of thinking about why the other person wouldn't want to speak with you, identify reasons why they would want to hear from you. Why do you avoid making the call? What is the biggest fear you have about using the phone?

_____

_____

_____

_____

_____

_____

_____

_____

_____

_____

_____

_____

_____

_____

_____

_____

_____

TIP: Making or receiving phone calls elicits a lot of fear in people with social anxiety, but you don't have to fear using the phone. Try easing into it by making a call to a number that you know will be a recording, then to a close friend or family member with whom you are comfortable talking. Work your way up to making the call that you fear.

INTERVIEWING
WITH PURPOSE

—

Smile, breathe, and go slowly.

—*Thich Nhat Hanh*

PROMPT: The company that you have been hoping to work for calls to tell you that they would like you to come in for an interview. How do you feel about interviewing? What impression would you like to give the employer? What is the best way to do this? How would your ideal interview go?

_____

_____

_____

_____

_____

_____

_____

_____

_____

_____

_____

_____

_____

_____

_____

_____

TIP: You don't have to be overly anxious for an important interview. Instead, be prepared. Get the address and go to the site prior to your interview day to eliminate the stress of not knowing where to go and park. Wear comfortable clothes. If timing allows, try exercising before the interview. When answering the questions, remember to breathe and take your time. It's better to be thoughtful about your answers than to blurt out the first thing that comes into your mind.

WEARING A BATHING SUIT WITH CONFIDENCE

—

To me, beauty is about being comfortable in your own skin. It's about knowing and accepting who you are.

—Ellen DeGeneres

PROMPT: Your kids are having a blast at the pool. They have asked you to come play with them several times, but you can't stop thinking about how you look in a bathing suit. How do you want them to feel about the way they look? What message are you sending your kids when you repeatedly won't play with them? What do you think you have missed out on by not being comfortable in a bathing suit?

_____

_____

_____

_____

_____

_____

_____

_____

_____

_____

_____

_____

_____

_____

_____

_____

_____

TIP: Try to stop focusing on what you think is wrong with your body and begin to celebrate what you like about the way you look. Choose a bathing suit that complements your body type and a color that is good for your skin tone. Accessorize with hats, sunglasses, etc. Don't let your bathing suit obsessions steal your memories.

HAVING A
GOOD MORNING

—

When you arise in the morning, think of
what a precious privilege it is to be alive—
to breathe, to think, to enjoy, to love.

—Marcus Aurelius

PROMPT: The alarm goes off at 6:00 a.m., and you immediately begin to feel your heart race. As the sun rises, so does your anxiety. What do you typically begin to think about when you wake up? What negative thought patterns do you have? How does your nighttime routine impact your morning?

_____

_____

_____

_____

_____

_____

_____

_____

_____

_____

_____

_____

_____

_____

TIP: Your evening routine can impact your sleep, as well as your stress level the next morning. Try a relaxing nighttime routine to prepare your body for restful sleep. Make a list before bedtime of everything you need to get done the next day. This way your mind can rest—it won't keep trying to remind you of things while you are sleeping. Also, avoid caffeine and sugar first thing in the morning, and try to meditate before starting your day. Make a choice to have a great day.

WASHING AWAY THE
FEAR OF GERMS

—

A sad soul can kill quicker than a germ.

—John Steinbeck

PROMPT: While attending an out-of-town conference, you notice that a lot of people are coughing and sneezing. It is flu season, and you begin to think about the flight home and what it will be like on the germ-filled, enclosed plane. What feelings do you have when you think about germs? How has your fear of germs negatively affected your life? What about your fear is irrational?

_____

_____

_____

_____

_____

_____

_____

_____

_____

_____

_____

_____

_____

_____

_____

_____

TIP: Begin to face your fear of germs slowly at first. The best way to overcome it is to pick something that is mildly uncomfortable and do that thing. For example, if you tend to wash your hands after you touch a door handle, try to wait longer than usual before washing. Do this until you are able to skip washing your hands after touching something. Then add another challenge once you have mastered that one. You don't have to be controlled by your fears.

BREATHING CALMLY
IN TIGHT SPACES

—

Do the thing you fear, and the death of fear is certain.

—*Ralph Waldo Emerson*

PROMPT: You are on vacation, feeling relaxed. At the hotel, you get into an empty elevator and begin going up. The elevator stops at a floor that isn't yours, and a large group of people get on, pushing you to the back. How will you manage this elevator ride? Write about some of your experiences in which you felt uncomfortable in a tight space. What could you have done differently in those situations to make it less uncomfortable?

_____

_____

_____

_____

_____

_____

_____

_____

_____

_____

_____

_____

_____

_____

_____

_____

_____

TIP: When confined in a small space, it is very easy to feel trapped and maybe even to panic. It's important, when in such unpredictable situations, for you to take slow, deep breaths in through your nose and out through your mouth. Try picking one visual cue to focus on and repeat "I am okay. Fear is just a feeling, and it will pass."

EMBRACING
SEPARATION ANXIETY

—

What a lovely surprise to finally discover
how unlonely being alone can be.

—Ellen Burstyn

PROMPT: Your spouse leaves for work, and you have already begun texting and calling, even though you are trying not to. You feel the need to know where they are whenever they are not with you. What does being separated from someone or a pet mean to you? Why do you think you feel that way? What are some ways to begin to be more comfortable with separation?

_____

_____

_____

_____

_____

_____

_____

_____

_____

_____

_____

_____

_____

_____

TIP: Typically, separation anxiety is associated with children. However, adults can also suffer from an intense fear of separation from a loved one or pet. This fear may stem from a traumatic event in the past, or it could be a result of having an anxiety disorder. If your separation anxiety stems from a traumatic event, you should consider seeing a therapist to work through the trauma first. Regardless, you can begin to get more comfortable by meditating and engaging in activities that bring you joy while separated.

ROCKING THE DREADED DEADLINE

—

The gratifying feeling that our duty has been done.

—*W. S. Gilbert*

PROMPT: You are working on a project, and your boss has given you a strict deadline. You begin to worry over the outcome. How do you react to deadlines? What conditions do you work the best under? What is your ideal working atmosphere, and in what ways can you adjust your current situation to make it be more productive?

TIP: Some people thrive on deadlines, while others can get overwhelmed. Here are some ways you can make deadlines work for you: Start by making a list of the tasks involved, and prioritizing what needs to be done. Identify what times of day or night you are most productive and schedule higher-priority items during those times. Set up a reward system for yourself in which you allow yourself an indulgence when you complete a task. Take breaks and be sure to not watch the clock. Stop focusing on ALL that needs to be done. Just focus on one task at a time, and you will rock that deadline!

SAYING NO TO
THE SCALE

—

No one can make you feel inferior without your consent.

—*Eleanor Roosevelt*

PROMPT: Your alarm goes off, and you sleepily walk to the scale, a ritual you do every morning and then several times throughout the day. Do you allow what the scale says to set the mood for your day or determine how much you will restrict your food intake? What does the number mean to you and why? Explore where your ideal body image came from. Try to keep it in perspective. If you found out that you or someone you loved were terminally ill, how important would your weight be? What would your life be like if you didn't check your weight so frequently?

TIP: The most important thing you can do to get over your obsession with weight is to change your mind-set. Too often, people are focused on a number, which may be unrealistic, instead of being healthy and happy. Begin by reducing the amount of times you weigh yourself until you are able to stop checking entirely. Set goals based on how you feel, rather than the number on the scale.

CHOOSING TO LIMIT
YOUR CHOICES

—

You can be crippled by too many choices, especially
if you don't know what your goals are.

—Chip Kidd

PROMPT: Your daughter wants to go shopping and takes you to a large discount store. There are many racks and tables of clothes. You begin to go through the clothing and see several items that you like, but when you look up, you see that you haven't even begun to look at everything the store has to offer. Write about a time that you felt over-whelmed in a store. How does having so many choices contribute to increased anxiety for you?

_____

_____

_____

_____

_____

_____

_____

_____

_____

_____

_____

_____

_____

_____

_____

_____

_____

_____

_____

_____

_____

TIP: Too many choices are difficult for people and can cause a spike in anxiety when they're faced with needing to make a decision. Therefore, it may be helpful to go into stores with a specific plan. Pick one or two items that you need, and try to avoid looking at everything all at once. Stay in the section that serves you, so you do not begin to get overwhelmed.

HAVING HAPPY
HOLIDAYS

—

*The greatest weapon against stress is our ability
to choose one thought over another.*

—*William James*

PROMPT: The holidays are approaching, and you are hosting your family. Write about what is the most stressful part of the holidays for you. What does your ideal holiday look like? What do you have control over?

TIP: The holidays are supposed to be a time for getting together with loved ones and being joyful. But for many, the holidays are a time of pressure, stress, and anxiety. Identifying what makes the holidays so stressful is the best place to start. Is it the planning, the money spent, the dealing with family? Figure out what you can do ahead of time and also what you can take off your plate. Ask yourself if everything you are doing is necessary, or if you are able to delegate some duties. Start planning early and make a decision to enjoy yourself.

ASKING, "ARE MY KIDS GOOD ENOUGH?"

—

Most people who are criticizing and judging
haven't even tried what you failed at.

—David Goggins

PROMPT: You are having coffee with your friends after school drop-off, and you begin discussing a child in your son's grade who recently made a poor choice. The conversation turns to judging the way the child's parents handled the situation. When you hear others being critical about parenting styles, or when you are judging someone else's parenting style, how do you feel about your own parenting? Write about how you contribute to your own insecurity as a parent. Do you care too much about what your peers think of your parenting and your child? Do you allow your child's behavior to define what kind of parent you are?

_____

_____

_____

_____

_____

_____

_____

_____

_____

_____

_____

_____

_____

_____

_____

_____

_____

_____

TIP: Every child is different and requires different parenting. It's not fair for others to judge parenting choices that you make. By judging others, you perpetuate your own insecurity and need for approval. Focus on the moments that you are with your child and their needs, not on your friends' approval.

MEDITATIONS

QUIET YOUR MIND
MEDITATION

—

Be present in all things, and thankful for all things.

—Maya Angelou

Sometimes it's hard to turn off your mind. It's important to give your racing mind a rest and refocus on what is important and within your control. This meditation is designed to help you clear your mind and focus on the present.

TIME: 10 minutes

Turn off all devices and anything else that may distract you.

Find a quiet, comfortable spot.

Place one hand on your chest and one hand on your stomach.

When you take a deep breath in, focus on filling your stomach with air and feeling the hand on your stomach rise. Hold for a moment and slowly exhale.

Repeat this 5 to 10 times, or as many times as you need, to slow your heart rate and begin to relax.

Identify 5 things you can see.

Touch 4 different items.

Identify 3 things you can hear.

Identify 2 things you can smell.

Identify 1 thing you can taste.

Close your eyes and continue taking deep breaths. Repeat in your mind, "I am present. I am in control."

RESTORATIVE SLEEP MEDITATION

—

When I wake up, I am reborn.

—Mahatma Gandhi

Truly restful sleep is a gift, not often given to individuals who suffer from anxiety. This meditation will help you fall asleep with a clear mind, so you can get restorative sleep.

TIME: 15–20 minutes

Get into a comfortable position and close your eyes.

Take a deep breath and let it out slowly.

Focus on your breath going in and out.

Inhale for a slow count of 4, hold for a count of 7, and exhale for a count of 8.

It's okay if your mind drifts. When you notice that happening, simply refocus on your breathing.

Do this until you gently fall asleep.

TREAT YOURSELF WITH LOVE AND KINDNESS MEDITATION

—

The present moment is filled with joy and happiness. If you are attentive, you will see it.

—Thich Nhat Hanh

As you live your life, you have many experiences that shape who you are and how you treat yourself, as well as how you allow others to treat you. Use this meditation to help you love yourself the way you deserve to be loved.

TIME: 15 minutes

Before beginning this meditation, find a photograph of yourself when you were a toddler or young child. Have the picture with you and take a moment to look at your younger self before beginning.

Find a comfortable position and begin to become aware of your breathing.

Once your breathing has slowed and you begin to feel relaxed, imagine that child in the picture in your mind.

Visualize taking their hand and begin to take a walk, paying attention to how the child's hand feels in yours.

Find a comfortable place to sit down on your walk and look the child in the eyes.

Tell the child that you love them. That you won't let anyone mistreat them, and that it is your job to take care of them.

Spend some time with the child, talking about whatever you want to talk about and promising that you will treat them with respect and love, always.

When you are done, give the child a long hug and slowly open your eyes. Take a picture of your photograph and keep it in your phone, as a screensaver, or somewhere that you will see it often to remind yourself daily of your promise to love and care for yourself.

BEATING OBSESSIVE THOUGHTS MEDITATION

—

Surrender to what is. Let go of what
was. Have faith in what will be.

—Sonia Ricotti

Everyone experiences intrusive thoughts, but sometimes the thoughts can be difficult to ignore or may begin to interfere with your happiness. Use this meditation when you start to have intrusive thoughts.

TIME: 10 minutes

Find a comfortable place and close your eyes.

Notice your breathing without trying to control it.

Breathe in through your nose and out through your mouth.

Allow the intrusive thought to enter your mind.

Don't fight the feelings that the thought brings. Instead, notice how you feel. Tell yourself that this is just a feeling and it will pass. The thought does not control you. You control your thoughts.

Put the thought into a bubble and watch it float away.

PROGRESSIVE RELAXATION MEDITATION

—

Sometimes the most productive thing you can do is to step outside and do nothing . . . Relax and enjoy nature.

—Melanie Charlene

Use progressive relaxation as a way to slowly become aware of the tension and stress in your body, and begin to let it go.

TIME: 10–15 minutes

Lie down in a comfortable position and close your eyes.

Become aware of your breathing, in and out.

Notice the tips of your toes, and mentally scan your entire body slowly. Move to the arch in your feet, then your heel, and begin to move up to your calves.

Scan your entire body in your mind, moving in a slow progression upward.

Become aware of your body and where it is touching the surface beneath you.

Feel the tension release as you become aware of each area of your body.

QUICK MEDITATION WHEN YOU DON'T HAVE MUCH TIME

—

Do not anticipate trouble, or worry about what may never happen. Keep in the sunlight.

—Benjamin Franklin

It's important to fit meditation into your daily routine, but some days you might just feel as if you don't have time. Use this quick meditation if you have only a few minutes.

TIME: 5 minutes

Sit upright with both feet on the floor.

Close your eyes.

Take a big deep breath in, and as you exhale, imagine all of your stress and worries leaving your body.

In your mind, say the word "mantra" with each inhale. Exhale your stress.

Do this for 5 minutes.

PUBLIC SPEAKING MEDITATION

—

It usually takes me more than three weeks to prepare for a good impromptu speech.

—*Mark Twain*

When preparing to speak in public, it's important to not only know your content, but also to prepare your body and mind. Practice this meditation in the days leading up to the event to best prepare for a confident presentation.

TIME: 15–20 minutes

Sit upright in a chair and become aware of your breath.

Close your lips. Inhale deeply through your nose to a count of 4.

Hold for a count of 7.

Exhale through your mouth for a count of 8.

Imagine yourself giving your presentation from start to finish; speaking slowly, loudly, and clearly, and projecting confidence throughout the talk.

Do this meditation every day leading up to your presentation.

ANXIETY-FREE DRIVING/BRIDGES MEDITATION

—

The cave you fear to enter holds the treasure you seek.

—Joseph Campbell

The best way to overcome your fear of driving or of bridges is to slowly expose yourself to them. Adding a meditation to the process will help you conquer your fear faster.

TIME: 10–15 minutes

Begin this meditation with 4–7–8 breathing as you would in the Public Speaking Meditation (page 156).

Read the list of positive outcomes from driving that you created in your journal. Pick a few of your sentences and slowly repeat them in your head.

For example, "Driving allows me to be in control of where I go and when I go somewhere."

Keep your breathing slow and steady.

Add this meditation to your gradual exposure to driving.

RISING ANXIETY IN SOCIAL SETTINGS MEDITATION

—

Be who you are and say what you feel, because those who
mind don't matter and those who matter don't mind.

—Dr. Seuss

If you are in a social setting and begin to feel anxiety creeping in,
simply excuse yourself to the bathroom and practice this meditation.

TIME: Any amount of time needed

Begin by running your hands under cold water, then placing them on your face and neck.

Close your eyes.

Place one hand on your stomach and one on your chest.

Inhale deeply through your mouth and fill your stomach with air until you see the hand on your stomach rise.

Try to keep the hand on your chest still. You are filling your belly with air, not your lungs.

Repeat this several times until your heart rate slows.

I AM GRATEFUL
MEDITATION

—

There is a calmness to a life lived in gratitude, a quiet joy.

—*Ralph H. Blum*

Focusing on the things you are grateful for allows your mind to calm and find happiness, instead of focusing on what upsets you or what you don't have. Try a gratitude exercise each day.

TIME: 20–30 minutes

Find a comfortable spot. You can either lie down or sit upright for this meditation.

Take a deep breath, and as you exhale notice how your body feels. Spend a few minutes relaxing and focusing on the present moment. What sounds do you hear? What do you feel? Are there any smells?

Take a moment to think about the people in your life whom you love.

Make a list in your mind of everyone you love and why you are grateful for them.

Think about your day today. Which people did you encounter for whom you are grateful? The garbage collector for taking your trash? The gardener who plants flowers in town?

What are the things that you are grateful for that you can do?

> *Examples:*
> *I am grateful for two legs that work and that allow me to walk.*
> *I am grateful for my education.*

Once you spend time going through things and people you are grateful for, become aware of your surroundings.

What do you hear, feel, smell?

Slowly open your eyes and find one thing you see that you are grateful for. Maybe it's the sun shining or your dog next to you.

Make a decision to have a great day.

MEDITATION
FOR OBSESSIVE
THOUGHTS

—

You can't stop the waves, but you can learn to surf.

—Jon Kabat-Zinn

Everybody experiences obsessive thoughts at times. When you realize that you are ruminating on a topic, try to take a few minutes and meditate to refocus your mind.

TIME: 10 minutes

Get comfortable and notice your breath going in and out.

Imagine ahead of you is a tall, green, grassy hill. As you begin to slowly walk up the hill, you feel the warm sun on your face and a slight breeze go through your hair.

With every step up the hill, you are becoming more relaxed. You notice the tension in your body start to leave. Feel yourself relax more and more with each step. You may even begin to feel sleepy.

When you reach the top, take a deep breath in and hold it for 5 seconds, then exhale through your mouth.

Recall the thought you were obsessing about. Allow it to enter your mind without fighting it. Tell the thought that you will not be controlled by it any longer. Thoughts cannot hurt you. They may make you uncomfortable, but you are safe. The feeling will pass. Focus on breathing in, holding for 5 seconds, and exhaling. Repeat until the anxiety has passed.

TAKING A TEST WITH
EASE MEDITATION

—

*Your mind will answer most questions if you
learn to relax and wait for the answer.*

—*William S. Burroughs*

Visualizing success can be very powerful. In the days leading up to
your test or exam, use this meditation to help you reframe your anxiety
about test taking. Additionally, use this meditation right before you take
the test, if possible.

TIME: 15 minutes

Get into a comfortable position in a place with no distractions. Wear comfortable clothes and get a blanket if you need one.

Begin by taking a deep breath in, filling your stomach with air, then slowly exhaling.

In and out.

In and out.

Imagine yourself feeling confident, prepared, and excited to take the test.

Imagine what the room looks like and see yourself walking in.

You are rested, aware, and feeling good.

Now imagine answering the questions on the test, slowly and thoughtfully. You are confident and knowledgeable.

Take a deep breath in and slowly exhale.

Take your time to fully complete the test in your mind and turn it in with pride.

Take another deep breath in, and open your eyes as you exhale.

COUNT YOUR WAY TO
SLEEP MEDITATION

—

Feelings come and go like clouds in a windy
sky. Conscious breathing is my anchor.

—Thich Nhat Hanh

Being able to fall asleep is a gift. It's also important to get restful sleep in order to live a healthy lifestyle. Try these meditations to see which ones work best for you.

TIME: 10–15 minutes, or however long it takes

Before you begin this meditation, sit and write down all the thoughts you have running through your mind, like what you don't want to forget for tomorrow and any lists that need to get made. This allows your mind to be clear, knowing that you won't forget your to-dos because you have written them down.

Find a comfortable sleeping position. Begin by slowly inhaling through your nose for a count of 4, holding your breath for a count of 7, and exhaling to a count of 8. Repeat this 4–7–8 breathing until you feel your heart rate slow and you begin to relax.

Take notice of your body, including its heaviness in the bed. Scan your body from the top of your head to your toes. Feel each part of your body release tension.

Focus on the number 1 in your mind. See it as you inhale, and as you exhale, visualize it blowing away like a cloud. Now picture the number 2—inhale slowly and blow it away with your exhale.

It's okay if your mind wanders. Just bring your attention back to your numbers until you fall into a deep, restful sleep.

QUICK PROGRESSIVE RELAXATION MEDITATION

—

Sometimes the most important thing in a whole day
is the rest we take between two deep breaths.

—*Etty Hillesum*

Throughout your day, you may notice tension building in your neck, head, and shoulders. Take a few minutes to release this tension, and then continue your day more aware of your relaxed body.

TIME: less than 5 minutes

Begin by taking a deep breath in and exhaling. Take another breath and hold it. Then exhale.

Raise your shoulders up to your ears and hold the tension as tight as you can without pain. Slowly release your shoulders, feeling the tension leave. Repeat, this time with your hands clenched, then release. Next, tighten your face, eyebrows, eyes, and lips, and then slowly release the tension from each of these areas. Your body will be free of the tension that you were building, and you will be ready to take on the rest of your day.

STOPPING PANIC
MEDITATION

—

You're worried about what-ifs. Well,

what if you stopped worrying?

—*Shannon Celebi*

Having a panic attack can be very scary. It can even feel as if you were
having a heart attack. But always remember that the panic will end.
Panic lasts only for a certain amount of time, and then it goes away.
It can't hurt you. Use this meditation to bring yourself back from panic.

TIME: 10–20 minutes

Take a big breath in and hold it for a moment. Slowly exhale.

Take another breath in, and this time, fill your stomach with air and hold it. Then exhale.

Repeat this breathing sequence as many times as you need to, until you start to feel your body relax—your shoulders release, your fists unclench, your neck loosens.

Remind yourself that anxiety is just a feeling. It passes and it will not harm you. Repeat in your mind or say out loud:

I am safe.
This will pass.
I am okay.

Keep breathing and repeating the words until you are calm and feel like yourself again.

■ *about the author*

Brandi Matz, MSW, LCSW, has spent the last 20 years working in a variety of settings, including inpatient, residential, outpatient, and private practice and has been a consultant for New Jersey alternative schools. She currently has a full-time private practice specializing in anxiety, where she provides in-office as well as online therapy. Most recently, she developed an online, interactive therapeutic course focused on the best strategies to manage anxiety, allowing individuals to access help anywhere in the world, at their own pace. Brandi resides in Connecticut with her husband and children. To learn more, she can be found at BrandiMatz.com.

CPSIA information can be obtained
at www.ICGtesting.com
Printed in the USA
JSHW020840070820
7168JS00001B/3